Wyoming Fish Species

Game Fish & Panfish

Billy Grinslott & Kinsey Marie Books

ISBN - 9781965098837

Chubs and Shiners are two types of minnows that are considered panfish. There are several types of shiners and chubs. Many people will use them as bate to catch larger fish. Here's a list of some. Bigmouth shiner, Emerald shiner. Golden shiner, Lake chub, Utah chub, Sturgeon chub, Roundtail chub

The Green Sunfish is blue green in color. It has yellow flecks on both its scales and some parts of its sides. The Green Sunfish also has broken blue stripes which is why some people confuse it with the Bluegill. Green Sunfish are very adaptable, they can live in any body of water that has vegetation or weeds.

Sculpins are small, bottom-dwelling fish with a flattened body shape, large pectoral fins, and a unique camouflage pattern, often found in clear, fast-flowing waters with rocky substrates, and they are known for their ambush hunting tactics. Sculpins have very large mouths and can swallow items nearly as large as themselves.

The burbot, also known as the eel pout. They get their name because they have a serpent-like or eel-like body. They can wrap their tail around things. There's nothing to worry about if you catch one, they may try to wrap their tail around your arm, but they are harmless. Burbots are adapted to cold water and are found in large, cold rivers, lakes, and reservoirs, primarily preferring freshwater habitats. Burbots are also known as eelpout, lingcod, and lawyer. The largest burbot caught in Wyoming weighed 19.25 pounds and measured 44 inches.

The bluegill also considered a sunfish is the most popular fish to fish for. They are called pan fish because they are about the size of a frying pan. Bluegills love to eat insects and bugs. They have good vision and rely on their keen eyesight to feed. Three types in this group are the Bluegill, Sunfish, and Pumpkinseed.

The Pumpkinseed is also known as pond perch, sun perch, and punky's sunfish. It can be found in numerous lakes, ponds, and rivers. It is their body shape resembling the seed of a pumpkin, that inspired their name. Pumpkinseed sunfish have speckles on their orangish colored sides and back, with a yellow to orange belly and chest. Pumpkinseeds can be found in Wyoming, particularly in warmwater fisheries like Sloan's Lake in Cheyenne and other similar habitats.

The Rock Bass is not actually a bass but a member of the sunfish family. The biggest Rock Bass ever caught on record weighs about three pounds and was a little over one foot long. Rock bass prefer waters with rocky vegetated areas, that's how they got their name. They have been found in the river drainages and have moved downstream into southern Wyoming.

There are two main types of crappies. The white crappie and the black crappie. They are also members of the sunfish family. The difference between the white and black crappie is one has dark spots and the other has dark lines and is lighter in color. The white crappie has six dorsal fin spines, whereas the black crappie has eight dorsal fin spines. The white crappie can grow bigger and more of the bigger white crappie are caught in North America.

The two most famous perches are the common perch and the yellow perch. The yellow perch has a brilliant greenish yellow color with orange fins. The yellow perch is the biggest one and can grow to a size of 18 inches. It's also known as the jumbo perch. The other type of perch is the white perch. The Wyoming Game and Fish Department discovered yellow perch in Saratoga Lake in 2021.

White Bass range in color from a silvery white to a pale green. Their backs are mostly black, while their sides and belly are pale with stripes running along them. White Bass are related to Striped Bass and called wipers. White bass are present in some Wyoming, particularly in the Snake River drainage and other areas with suitable conditions.

Goldeye fish typically average around 12 inches in length and weigh about 1 pound but can grow up to 20 inches long. Their most distinctive feature is their yellow or gold-colored eyes. Their yellow or gold-colored eyes are adapted for low-light conditions and allows them to see when the water is darker. Goldeye are also known as mooneye.

Whitefish are related to salmon and trout. They are known for their deep-bodied, silvery appearance and are a major part of the lake's ecosystem. They typically grow to 17-22 inches and range from 1.5-4 pounds. Whitefish are a popular and valuable commercial fish, generating income for commercial fisheries. Whitefish are also known as, whiting, and shad.

The largemouth bass is the most sought-after bass in North America. Largemouth bass live in just about every lake in North America. They have great hearing and can hear a crayfish crawling on the bottom of the lake. The largest largemouth bass caught in Wyoming weighed 11.51 pounds.

Smallmouth bass have a smaller mouth than the largemouth bass. They also have different markings and are lighter in color. They prefer living in colder water. They are typically found in the northern states in America because the water is cooler. The current world record smallmouth is an 11-pound, 15-ounce fish caught in Dale Hollow Lake. They can be found in lakes, reservoirs, and rivers. The largest smallmouth bass caught in Wyoming weighed 5.94 pounds.

Male freshwater drum make a rumbling or grunting sound by contracting muscles along their air bladder walls. They have large, ivory-like ear bones that can be up to an inch in diameter, which Native Americans used as necklaces or bracelets and sometimes referred to as the lucky stones. Freshwater drum are primarily bottom feeders, spending much of their time near the bottom of lakes and rivers in search of food. The largest freshwater drum caught in Wyoming weighed 22.58 pounds, Length 34 inches.

Buffalo Fish are sometimes confused with carp. Buffalo fish have a downward-facing mouth, capable of sucking bits of food out of the silt and sand on the bottom. They have broad bodies, blunt heads, and silvery gray or brown scales. Buffalo fish are members of the suckerfish family. Bigmouth buffalo fish can be found in the eastern portion of the state. The largest bigmouth buffalo caught in Wyoming weighed 11.51 pounds.

Carp have long been an important food fish to humans. Carp are bottom feeders for the most part and their mouth is made like a suction cup, so they can suck food off the bottom. Carp are good for a lake because they help clean the bottom of the lake. Carp can tolerate a wide range of water temperatures and low oxygen levels, allowing them to survive in a variety of habitats. Carp are considered an invasive species in many areas. The largest carp caught in Wyoming weighed 34 pounds 6.5 ounces.

The black bullhead and yellow bullhead are part of the catfish family. They usually only grow to about 10 inches long. They use their whiskers to help find food. The bullhead is the most common member of the catfish family. Bullheads live in the water containing low oxygen levels. They can survive on low oxygen areas, where other fish can't.

Flathead Catfish, their body is wide but flattened and very low in height. Both eyes are on the top of the flattened head, giving excellent vision to see upward. Flathead catfish live mainly in large bodies of water like big rivers and reservoirs. They prefer deep pools. The Wyoming record for a flathead catfish is 22.46 pounds and 34 inches in length.

There are a couple other different types of catfish in Wyoming, the channel and the stonecat. The Channel Catfish are the most fished catfish species with around 8 million anglers fishing for them per year. Channel Catfish have very few teeth and swallow their food whole. Channel catfish live in freshwater rivers, lakes, streams, and ponds. Catfish can live in low oxygen water, like bullheads. The largest channel catfish ever caught in Wyoming weighed 28.52 pounds, was 39 inches long.

There are several types of sucker fish in Wyoming. The White sucker, River carpsucker, Utah sucker, Longnose sucker. bluehead suckers, green suckers and Flannelmouth Suckers. Sucker fish feed off the bottom with their suction cup shaped mouth. The official weight of the new longnose sucker record was 2 pounds, 4.5 ounces. The length of the fish was 18 inches.

Redhorse fishes are part of the sucker family and are known for their bottom-facing mouths and fleshy lips which they use to suck food off the bottom. Redhorse has large, molar-like throat teeth that are an adaptation for crushing the shells of mollusks. redhorses construct nests in clean gravel, using their tails to sweep and their mouths to carry rocks or move materials with their heads.

Shovelnose Sturgeons have sharp spines on their back, so be careful when handling them. Instead of scales, sturgeon skin is covered in bony plates called scutes, which can be very sharp on young sturgeon. Sturgeons have been around since the dinosaur days. Sturgeons mostly live in large, freshwater lakes and rivers. Their average lifespan is 50 to 60 years. The largest shovelnose sturgeon caught in Wyoming, a state record, weighed 10 pounds and 4.2 ounces.

The sauger is part of the walleye family. There are 2 different types of saugers. The normal sauger and the suageye. The saugeye is a mix of the sauger and walleye. The suageye have white eyes just like the walleye. The sauger and suageye are smaller than the walleye. Sauger are found in portions of the Powder, Wind, and Bighorn rivers in Wyoming. The Wyoming record for a sauger is 7.50 pounds and 26.5 inches long.

The walleye got its name because of its white looking eyes. Their eyes collect light, even in low light conditions. This means they can see in the dark. Because they can see in the dark, they mostly feed at night. During the daytime their eyes are very sensitive, so they usually head for deeper water or shady places. Walleye like to live in cooler water and are normally found in the upper part of North America.Tthey are found in various lakes and reservoirs, including Grey Rocks Reservoir, Ocean Lake, and Glendo Reservoir. The Wyoming record for a walleye weighs 17.42 pounds.

The Northern Pike is one of the most sought-after fish for anglers. It got its name because it likes to live in cooler water mainly in the northern states of North America. The northern pike is a very aggressive predator. They don't like to live in groups with other fish, they are very territorial and like to live alone. Their behavior is closely affected by weather conditions. They are abundant in the Keyhole Reservoir, and other areas, like ponds near Sheridan. The largest Northern Pike caught in Wyoming weighed 27.4 pounds.

The tiger muskie is a cross between the northern pike and muskie. They grow larger and faster than normal muskies and northern pikes. The tiger muskie got its name because it has tiger like stripes. Tiger Muskies are very rare and hard to catch. Tiger muskie have been stocked in several Wyoming locations, including Badwater Pond, Middle Depression Reservoir, Lake Cameahwait, and Beck Lake. The Wyoming state record for a tiger muskie is a 37-pound, 14-ounces, length 49 inches long.

Mature Golden trout have a deep olive-green back that fades to bright gold on the sides, a vibrant red-orange lateral line, and black speckles near the tail. Golden trout are native to the remote waters at elevations of 6,000 to 10,000 feet. Golden trout, typically average 6 to 12 inches in length. The largest golden trout caught in Wyoming weighed 11.25 pounds.

The Cutthroat trout is Wyoming's state fish. The cutthroat's name comes from the bright red or orange slash-like markings under their jaws. There are several subspecies of cutthroat trout, including the coastal, Yellowstone, and Lahontan cutthroat. They inhabit a variety of cold, freshwater environments, including small streams, rivers, and lakes. Mature cutthroat trout can range from 6 to 40 inches in length. The largest cutthroat trout caught in Wyoming weighed 15 pounds, length was 32 inches.

Bull trout thrive in cold, clean, and complex aquatic habitats, with water temperatures ideally below 55°F. Some bull trout are anadromous, meaning they migrate from freshwater to saltwater for part of their life cycle, and then return to freshwater to spawn. Bull trout usually grow to a common length of around 25 inches, with the maximum reported length being 40.5 inches. They are found in high-alpine lakes and streams. The largest bull trout caught in Wyoming is 12.77-pounds, Length 31.25 inches.

Yellowstone cutthroat trout, a native species in Wyoming, are distinguished by prominent red slashes on their lower jaws, large black spots, and orange to drab coloration. They inhabit relatively clear, cold streams, rivers, and lakes. They typically measure from 6 to 30 inches long when they reach maturity. In August 2020 a Yellowstone cutthroat trout set a new state catch and release record with a length of 30.5-inches.

Ohrid trout are native to Ohrid Lake in Macedonia. The US Fish and Wildlife Service imported them to the US in 1965, including to Wyoming, because of their tendency to spawn in lakes. Ohrid trout have been stocked in some Wyoming waters, including Viva Naughton Reservoir on the Green River, lakes near Casper, and the North Platte River. They are characterized by a fusiform body with silvery coloration and numerous black spots. The largest Ohrid trout caught in Wyoming, and a world record, weighed 14 pounds and 4 ounces.

Brown trout can live up to 20 years. Brown trout have higher tolerance for warmer waters than either brook or rainbow trout. Brown trout can be found on almost every continent except Antarctica, and many can be found living in the ocean. The largest brown trout caught in Wyoming weighed 25 pounds and 13 ounces and was 34-1/4 inches long

Brook trout are characterized by their olive-green bodies with pale, worm-like markings, red spots with bluish halos, and orange-red fins with white and black edges. They can grow up to 12 inches in length. Brook trout are cold-water fish that prefer clean, clear, and cold streams, lakes, and ponds. The largest brook trout caught in Wyoming weighed 9 pounds, 11 ounces.

In Wyoming, the primary salmon species you'll find are landlocked sockeye salmon, also known as kokanee. These are the non-anadromous form of sockeye salmon, meaning they don't migrate to the ocean. They live their entire lives in freshwater lakes and reservoirs. The largest kokanee salmon caught in Wyoming weighed 14 pounds.

The Arctic grayling is one of the most beautiful freshwater fishes. Its most striking physical feature is the large, sail like dorsal or backfin. The Arctic grayling comes in a wide array of colors. Their color can vary from stream to stream. The sides of the body, fins and head can be freckled with spots. They can grow to be 30 inches long and weigh up to 8.4 pounds. They can travel more than 100 miles in one year. The largest Arctic grayling caught in Wyoming weighed 2.36 pounds.

The lake trout is one of the biggest of the trout family. The biggest lake trout caught was 72 pounds. Lake trout like to live in lakes that are deep. They like being in the cool water in the deep parts of a lake. They have been reported to live up to 70 years in some Canadian lakes. The largest lake trout caught in Wyoming weighed 50 pounds.

Fun Facts About Wyoming Fish

1 - The cutthroat trout was designated the official state fish of Wyoming in 1987.

2 - Rainbow and Brown Trout were introduced to Wyoming waters, and are now widely dispersed.

3 - Shovelnose sturgeons are a smaller than other sturgeons, reaching lengths of 30 inches and weighing up to 5 pounds.

4 - The world-record golden trout was caught in Wyoming at 11 pounds in 1948.

5 - Wyoming has 4,200 lakes, 27,000 miles of rivers and streams, and 14 reservoirs, offering a wide variety of fishing.

6 - The first fishing season was set in 1884, and the first creel limit (bag limit) was in place at 20 pounds of trout by 1899.

7 - Lake trout are the largest fish that live in Wyoming, with a state record fish weighing fifty pounds.

Author Page

Billy Grinslott & Kinsey Marie Books

ISBN – 9781965098837

Thanks

www.ingramcontent.com/pod-product-compliance
Lightning Source LLC
Chambersburg PA
CBHW060852270326
41934CB00002B/110